CAPTURED
WORLD
HISTORY

CHE GUEVARA'S FACE

HOW A CUBAN PHOTOGRAPHER'S IMAGE BECAME A CULTURAL ICON

by Danielle Smith-Llera

Content Adviser: Daniel C. Hellinger, PhD
Professor of International Relations
Webster University

COMPASS POINT BOOKS
a capstone imprint

Compass Point Books are published by Capstone,
1710 Roe Crest Drive, North Mankato, Minnesota 56003
www.mycapstone.com

Editor: Catherine Neitge
Designers: Tracy Davies McCabe and Catherine Neitge
Media Researcher: Svetlana Zhurkin
Library Consultant: Kathleen Baxter
Production Specialist: Kathy McColley

Image Credits
Alamy: Heritage Image Partnership Ltd., 44, Julio Etchart, 55, 58; Andrea Altemüller,
35; AP Photo: Alan Diaz, 39, Prensa Latina, 5, 8, 30, 56, Revolucion/Korda, 29;
DVIC: NARA, 14; Getty Images: Bettmann, 17, The LIFE Picture Collection/Joseph
Scherschel, 19, Three Lions, 24, 57, Universal Images Group, 7; iStockphoto:
duncan1890, 13; Newscom: Everett Collection/CSU Archives, 18, 47, 59 (top),
imageBROKER/Egon Bömsch, 41, picture alliance/Peter Heinz Junge, 20, Polaris/
Noah Friedman-Rudovsky, 27, 59 (bottom), REX/Clive Dixon, 49, Universal Images
Group/Sovfoto, 23, World History Archive, 21, ZUMA Press/Keystone Pictures USA,
42; Shutterstock: Maurizio De Mattei, 37, monotoomono, 53, Saikat Paul, 50;
Wikimedia: Alberto Korda, cover, 9, 11, 33

Library of Congress Cataloging-in-Publication Data
Names: Smith-Llera, Danielle, 1971- author.
Title: Che Guevara's face : how a Cuban photographer's image became a cultural icon
/ by Danielle Smith-Llera.
Description: North Mankato, Minnesota : Compass Point Books, an imprint of
Capstone Press, [2017] | Series: CPB grades 4-8. Captured world history |
Includes bibliographical references and index. | Audience: Ages 10-15._
Identifiers: LCCN 2016008219| ISBN 9780756554408 (library binding) |
ISBN 9780756554422 (paperback) | ISBN 9780756554446 (ebook : pdf)
Subjects: LCSH: Korda, Alberto, 1928-2001. Guerillero heroico—Juvenile literature.
| Guevara, Che, 1928-1967—Portraits—Juvenile literature. | Guevara, Che,
1928-1967—Influence—Juvenile literature. | Guevara, Che, 1928-1967—In mass
media—Juvenile literature. | Guerrillas—Latin America—Biography—Juvenile
literature. | Cuba—History—1959-1990—Juvenile literature.
Classification: LCC F2849.22.G85 S525 2016 | DDC 972.9106/4092—dc23
LC record available at http://lccn.loc.gov/2016008219

Printed and bound in the USA.
009692F16

TABLEOFCONTENTS

ChapterOne:
TRAGEDY IN HAVANA

Stone angels bent over graves inside Havana's Colón Cemetery. Palm trees swayed against a gray sky on an unseasonably cold day for a Caribbean island. A block away, thousands of Cubans filled the streets, stunned with grief. Before them stood their country's leader, Prime Minister Fidel Castro, high on a stage built on a flatbed truck. Microphones boomed his voice over the crowd as he began: "There are moments of great importance in the life of a nation. There are minutes that are extraordinary. One of these is this moment, this tragic, bitter moment we are going through today."

Castro retold the terrible events of the day before, March 4, 1960. Dockworkers at Havana Harbor had been unloading a cargo of 76 tons (69 metric tons) of weapons from the French ship *La Coubre*. Suddenly an explosion had ripped through the ship, blowing debris across the harbor waters and alarming people across the city.

Thirty minutes later a second explosion had shaken the harbor. More than 200 had been wounded, many losing limbs. As many as 100 dockworkers, sailors, rescuers, and others had died, many of their bodies damaged beyond recognition.

Castro firmly believed the explosions had not been

Two explosions rocked Havana Harbor on March 4, 1960, causing speculation on who was behind the tragedy.

accidental, but sabotage. He declared that for the weapons "to explode, they must be set off." Castro told the crowd that the weapons were destroyed deliberately by "those who do not want our country to have defensive strength." He bellowed into the microphone, "We know our enemies!"

Holding exploded bomb casings, Castro accused the United States of attacking Havana Harbor.

"Do they want to frighten us?" he asked. Standing in front of a waving Cuban flag, he vowed, "Cuba will not be intimidated. "

In the audience, close to the stage, Alberto Korda pointed a camera up at Castro, taking photographs. He was on assignment for the newspaper *Revolución*. Korda's lens didn't stop moving for long. It traveled between Castro and two famous visiting French philosophers, the writers Jean-Paul Sartre and Simone de Beauvoir. Castro had invited them to sit on the stage, and they were listening intently.

Then Korda saw something unexpected in his viewfinder. The president of Cuba's Central Bank appeared, gazing out across the audience. He was 31-year-old Ernesto "Che" Guevara Lynch de la Serna, who had been among those who had rushed to *La Coubre* to help the victims.

"I saw him step forward with this absolute look of steely defiance as Fidel spoke," Korda said later. "It was only a brief moment that I had. I managed to shoot two frames and then he was gone."

There was good reason for Guevara to be on stage with Castro. They had been through much together. Earlier that day Korda had taken photos of both men leading a funeral procession for those killed in the harbor. Guevara and Castro wore military clothing and heavy boots, and they walked together with other government leaders, heads held high and arms linked

"It was only a brief moment that I had. I managed to shoot two frames and then he was gone."

Cuban leaders (from left) Fidel Castro, President Osvaldo Dorticós, Che Guevara, Augusto Martínez-Sánchez, and Antonio Nuñez-Jiménez walk arm in arm at the head of the funeral procession for victims of the *La Coubre* explosion.

like brothers. Behind them, people with bowed heads walked behind black hearses rolling along a wide seaside boulevard normally busy with cars.

Nearly the same age, Castro and Guevara shared a vision. Together they had helped topple a government under which Cuba's many poor people had not had any power.

For Castro, the *La Coubre* tragedy was proof that the United States not only disapproved of his new government—and its freedom to defend itself—but

Guevara (second from left), who was a physician, rushed to the scene of the *La Coubre* disaster in Havana.

was willing to attack his small island nation. Florida's coast was just 90 miles (145 kilometers) from its shores. He found no comfort in the fact that American officials had denied responsibility for the disaster. It is clear today that the U.S. Central Intelligence Agency began a sabotage campaign against Castro's government in the early 1960s, but no proof of U.S. involvement in the *La Coubre* explosion has surfaced. The cause of the blast remains a mystery.

Castro's two-hour speech lasted until dark. Korda

THE MAN BEHIND THE NEWSPAPER

Alberto Korda's contact sheet from March 5, 1960, includes his iconic portrait of Che Guevara.

Revolución editor Carlos Franqui did not choose Alberto Korda's photograph of Che Guevara for the March 6, 1960, edition of the paper. Franqui later explained: "It was the day after the *La Coubre* explosion. ... Obviously, [Castro] was the story, not Che." But Franqui helped make such photos possible.

Franqui, the first editor of the newspaper, said he wanted the pages to reflect the spirit of the revolution in a different way than the "olive green of Fidel and the rebel army." Through Franqui's connections with artists in Paris, new ideas about art traveled to Cuba. Cuba's citizens, even those who could not read, enjoyed the paper's bold design and large photographs. Its photographers and designers also worked to portray Cuba as friendly and attractive to other countries seeking alliances and trade partners.

But as Castro's government moved toward communism and stricter control of the newspaper, it became less tolerant of new ideas. Franqui quit in 1963 and left Cuba to live and work in Italy. In 1965 the Cuban government shut down three newspapers, including *Revolución*, and created its own government-run newspaper.

rushed to his studio to develop his film, hoping to deliver photographs to nearby newspaper offices that night. As the film was developed, a bearded Castro appeared many times. The French philosophers appeared, Sartre watching through thick glasses and de Beauvoir in a white head scarf. Guevara, standing alone, appeared in just two photos, his jacket zipped high and a beret over his long hair.

Carlos Franqui, *Revolución*'s editor, chose Korda's photographs of Castro and the French philosophers for the next day's edition of the paper. But Korda pinned a print of Guevara to his studio wall, where it remained for years, yellowing with age and tobacco smoke.

Who could have imagined that one day the photograph, which Korda called *Guerrillero Heroico (Heroic Guerrilla)*, would set out on a journey around the globe? Who would have expected it to become what has been called "the most famous photograph in the world and a symbol of the 20th century"?

Guerrillero Heroico (*Heroic Guerrilla*) would become world famous.

ChapterTwo
STRUGGLING FOR INDEPENDENCE

The small island nation of Cuba would seem to have been an unlikely threat to the United States. But less than three years after Castro blamed the United States for sabotaging its weapons, the world anxiously watched Cuba. The island's government nearly helped start a nuclear war.

For Cuban leaders in 1960, the *La Coubre* explosion was proof that powerful countries wanted to control life on the island, as they had for centuries. At the memorial service, Castro said Cuba must "defend its territory against enemies"—enemies who wanted to "keep us enslaved and starving."

Castro's suspicions were rooted in the troubled history of the nation. Spain controlled Cuba for nearly 400 years. Christopher Columbus sailed to Cuba's shores in 1492 and claimed the island for Spain. Spaniard Diego Velazquez soon began building a new colony. But colonists brutally disrupted the lives of the native Taino peoples who had farmed, hunted, and fished in Cuba for centuries. The Spanish forced the Taino to work for them and to endure cruel treatment. Most Taino died, either from Spanish weapons or European diseases. So the Spanish relied on the work of another group of people who had no freedom. Beginning in the early 1500s,

Surgarcane has played an important role in Cuba's economy for hundreds of years.

the Spanish brought enslaved Africans to the island.

Spain's rulers hoped the colony would provide great wealth. While they did not find golden riches, they did find fertile soil and a warm, wet climate. They introduced a new, lucrative crop to Cuba that would shape its history—sugarcane.

But Spain's relationship with its colony was tense. Cubans wanted freedom to shape their own government. They revolted in 1868, and struggled for years to be free of Spain. But it would take some last-minute help from another powerful nation to win.

The United States, rebuilt and thriving after its Civil War, was eager to push all other colonial powers out of the Americas and off the sugar-rich island of Cuba.

A mysterious explosion on another ship in Havana Harbor 62 years before the one on *La Coubre* pulled the United States into Cuba's war for independence. The USS *Maine* exploded on February 15, 1898, killing more than 250 men on board. Newspapers in the United States blamed Spain for attacking the ship. The U.S. public was horrified at the American sailors' deaths, and they were sympathetic toward the Cubans suffering under the Spanish.

The sinking of the USS *Maine* propelled the U.S. into the Spanish-American War.

The Cuban revolution grew into the Spanish-American War in April 1898. U.S. troops joined Cuban rebels. In December 1898 Spain, which was no match for the U.S. military, handed control of Cuba, along with Guam, Puerto Rico, and the Philippines, over to the United States. In 1934 the United States agreed to let Cuba govern itself. But Cuba depended on its powerful neighbor, which continued to buy most of the island's sugar at a high price. Wealthy Americans invested in Cuban businesses and spent large sums in the island's hotels and clubs. Luxury cars zoomed between parties in Havana.

But the lives of most Cubans—especially the people working in the countryside—remained difficult. Even though slavery in Cuba had been abolished in 1886, peasants earned very little money. Many of them worked on large plantations, called latifundios, owned by the wealthy. Americans and other foreigners owned about three-fourths of the farmland and more than half the sugar mills.

Cuba's elected leaders often used their power to increase their personal wealth. Former army officer Fulgencio Batista ignored elections and took over the government by force in 1952. He made deals with wealthy Cubans and foreign investors, including people involved in organized crime, to build hotels and casinos for gambling. Using political connections, he and his associates made millions of dollars.

For a young lawyer named Fidel Castro, Batista was an enemy of Cuba's poor. Castro led a failed attack on a barracks of Batista's soldiers on July 26, 1953. Castro was sent to prison and then into exile. But he did not give up the fight. While in Mexico in 1955, Castro met a young doctor who shared his passion for political ideas and his belief that only war could solve the plight of Cuba's poor people. The doctor was Che Guevara, who was visiting from Argentina. Together they would organize a revolution.

One November night in 1956, both men climbed into a small boat in Mexico with 80 armed men and sailed to Cuba. Batista's soldiers killed all but 19 of the poorly prepared fighters. The survivors retreated to the steep slopes of the Sierra Maestra in the eastern part of the island. There they recruited poor farmers to take up rifles—and even farm tools—to join them in a war against Batista's government.

Guevara served the Cuban Revolution as "Commandante Che." Cubans nicknamed him "Che" after the Argentine slang word for "buddy." Many admired his fearlessness in battle. They appreciated his care for the wounded, including enemy soldiers, with his medical training. For two years the world watched the revolution unfold with interest. Small groups of rebels were winning victories against larger numbers of Batista's troops. The rebels used

The only known photograph of Castro (center) and his rebel fighters at their secret base in Cuba. Also in the 1957 photo are Guevara (second from left) and Raúl Castro (kneeling).

surprise attacks and their knowledge of the island's jungles and mountains to defeat trained soldiers.

By New Year's Day 1959, the war was over and Batista had fled. Castro became prime minister, his brother Raúl was his deputy, and Guevara was third in command. The United States recognized Castro's new government. American leaders were pleased to see the unpopular and corrupt Batista overthrown. In the early months of the new government, Castro visited Washington, D.C., and met American leaders,

including Vice President Richard Nixon. Korda, who
accompanied Castro, captured the prime minister
in a photograph, gazing up at the Lincoln Memorial,
holding his military cap held behind his back.

Castro and his comrades still wore military
clothing because their revolution was not over.

Guevara, with his arm in a sling, in January 1959. He broke his arm shortly before the final battle of the revolution.

Batista was defeated, but his rich foreign friends who owned Cuban land and businesses remained. Cuba's new leaders were determined to end centuries of foreigners growing wealthy on the labor of the poor.

Castro, Guevara, and others considered the United States to be the enemy. They believed the powerful nation treated Cuba like a colony. About 80 percent of the money flowing into Cuba came from feeding the American appetite for sugar. Castro was frustrated that Cuba had remained "a one-crop economy ... an economy of an underdeveloped nation for 50 years." Cubans depended on U.S. food and manufactured goods, so Castro set high taxes on them. Cubans avoided buying these expensive products and U.S. businesses lost money.

Castro and others in his socialist government also found enemies inside Cuba. They believed that business owners were too powerful and insensitive to the lives of the poor. In 1960 Castro's government nationalized the sugar industry, taking over hundreds of large, privately owned farms and companies, many of which belonged to Americans. The owners received nothing for their property. As a result of Castro's policies, many upper-class and middle-class Cubans fled Cuba to start new lives in the U.S.

Cuba's bold actions shocked the United States. Its capitalist system gave private businesses freedom to compete for profits. But Castro believed his socialist

Castro believed
that nationalizing
the sugar industry
was good for the
Cuban people.

government was protecting Cubans from abuses suffered for centuries. "In the past the people had nothing," he said. "Today everything belongs to the people!"

The United States lost faith in Castro. He had taken political power without elections. He had executed hundreds of Batista's supporters.

Guevara putted the ball as Castro looked on in a golf game in Havana. It was said to have been played to make fun of President Eisenhower, an avid golfer.

Cubans who criticized the government risked arrest and imprisonment. President Dwight D. Eisenhower threatened to stop buying Cuban sugar. In late October 1959, he quietly began to help Castro's opponents.

Cuba once again turned to a foreign power for help. The Soviet Union promised to help Cuba fulfill a dream—one held passionately by Guevara, the new minister of labor—of becoming more than a sugar producer. In February 1960 both countries announced a new trade relationship: Cuba would sell sugar to the Soviet Union, and the Soviets would support Cuba with oil, grain, factories, and credit.

Cuba was playing a dangerous game by making an alliance with the United States' greatest enemy. Since World War II, various countries had been drawn into the conflict between the two superpowers, which was called the Cold War. The United States and the Soviet Union did not fight face-to-face but supported opposing combatants around the world. Cuba was about to become another Cold War battlefield.

If the Soviet Union was now Cuba's ally, then the United States was its enemy. Cuba scrambled to buy weapons. Castro explained that Cuba needed "to obtain the necessary weapons to answer an attack, to defend ourselves, to defend the rights of our people." They struggled to find a country willing to sell them and risk provoking the United States. So when *La Coubre* and its cargo of mostly Belgian rifles and grenades mysteriously exploded on March 4, 1960, Castro believed the United States was behind it.

The *La Coubre* tragedy pushed Cuba and the United States down a perilous path. At the memorial, Castro had shouted "Patria o muerte! Venceremos!" ("My homeland or death! We will win!") Now Castro asked the Soviet Union for more than industrial machines—he wanted weapons. Soviet premier

Cuba was playing a dangerous game by making an alliance with the United States' greatest enemy.

Fidel Castro met with Nikita Khrushchev (fist held high) during a four-week visit to the Soviet Union in the early 1960s.

Nikita Khrushchev eagerly agreed to arm an ally so close to his enemy.

The relationship between Cuba and the United States crumbled. In October 1960 President Eisenhower nearly ended U.S. trade by allowing only some U.S. food and medical supplies to travel to the island. The United States then closed the door to direct communication with Cuba. The United States brought down its flag on January 4, 1961, and it closed the U.S. Embassy in Havana.

At the *La Coubre* memorial, Castro had warned that the island nation could be "invaded at any time"

by its neighbor. On April 17, 1961, it happened. The United States had trained and armed 1,400 Cubans who had fled to the United States after Castro took over. They now returned to the shores of their homeland in an attempt to defeat Castro. But Castro's forces trapped the men on beaches near La Bahia de Cochinos, the Bay of Pigs. In less than a day of fighting, more than 100 of the U.S.-trained forces were killed, and more than 1,000 were taken prisoner.

The following year the United States used its most powerful diplomatic weapon against Cuba. President

John F. Kennedy approved a trade embargo on Cuba. The United States would no longer buy Cuban sugar, and no U.S. goods would enter the island. Daily life for Cubans changed dramatically. There was less food. There were no replacements for cars, telephones, and televisions when they broke. The island was more isolated than ever before.

A desperate Cuba—worried about another possible U.S. invasion—increased its dependence on the Soviet Union. The effects of the alliance would nearly be catastrophic for the world. In October 1962, a U.S. spy plane flying over Cuba discovered shocking evidence that the Soviets were building missile bases. Soviet nuclear weapons could now reach many major U.S. cities in less than five minutes—just as American nuclear weapons could quickly reach Soviet territory from nearby bases.

President Kennedy imposed a blockade to keep Soviet ships from delivering weapons and missiles to Cuba. In no uncertain terms, Kennedy demanded that the Soviet Union remove nuclear weapons so dangerously close to U.S. cities. For nearly two weeks, the world waited to see whether the weapons in Cuba would trigger nuclear war. American schoolchildren practiced bomb drills, ducking under their desks to be ready if missiles were launched.

But an agreement was reached, and the Cuban missile crisis ended quietly. The Soviet Union removed its missiles from Cuba, and the United States removed its missiles from a base close to the Soviet Union in Turkey. But the bitterness between the United States and Cuba remained. Cuba established its own communist party and moved closer to the Soviet Union. For decades the United States refused to lift the embargo.

But the two nations slowly made peace. The Cold War ended with the breakup of the Soviet Union in 1991. After Hurricane Michelle heavily damaged the island in 2001, Cuba bought food from the United States for the first time in 40 years. The two countries re-established full diplomatic relations in 2015. Cuba reopened its embassy in Washington, D.C., and U.S. Marines raised the Stars and Stripes over the reopened U.S. Embassy in Havana. In 2016 President Barack Obama became the first U.S. president to visit Cuba in 88 years.

Despite great challenges and controversy, Cuba has survived as an independent nation. Castro led the country until 2008 when his brother Raúl became president. For more than 45 years, however, it has been the face of their long-dead comrade Che Guevara, as captured by Korda, which has represented the spirit of revolution inside Cuba and around the world.

An image of Che Guevara seemed to gaze on President Barack Obama during his historic visit to Cuba in 2016.

ChapterThree
A REVOLUTIONARY IMAGE

Throughout his life Alberto Korda took little credit for his world-famous photograph of Che Guevara. He said that "it was snapped on the spur of the moment, a coincidence." Yet the power of the photograph, and its effect on the world, was hardly accidental.

Korda was taking photographs for a newspaper. But he was not simply a newspaper photographer on assignment at the memorial, pressing his way through the crowd to get close to the action. His position near the stage showed a special relationship with Fidel Castro. Korda had spent a decade as Castro's personal photographer, taking thousands of photographs. While working in Cuba, U.S. photographer Lee Lockwood observed that Korda was "the photographer of choice whenever Fidel wanted one around."

Korda dutifully photographed Cuba's leaders giving speeches at formal events. Yet he felt his best photographs captured "natural moments." He photographed Castro and Che fishing, playing chess, in deep discussion, or laughing in a cloud of cigar smoke. He even took pictures of Castro on a trip to the Soviet Union playing in the snow with Soviet premier Nikita Khrushchev. The photos were taken at about the time of the Cuban missile crisis.

Korda photographed Castro in 1962 in the Sierra Maestro. The Cuban leader revisted the mountainous area where the revolution started in the 1950s.

When Che unexpectedly stepped into Korda's viewfinder on the memorial stage, the photographer discovered a natural moment, despite the formality of the event. He later remembered being startled by Che's spontaneous expression. Only a soft glow through the clouds provides light in Korda's photo. Castro depended on the natural look favored by Korda and other photographers at the time. They worked with small 35mm cameras and no flashbulbs,

just natural light. Their photos told the story of Cuba's progress to its citizens—and to the watching world—in a simple and appealing way. They filled the pages of *Revolución* with images of average citizens harvesting sugarcane and working in factories.

At the *La Coubre* memorial service, Korda, as usual, was working with simple tools. His lightweight Leica M2 was an affordable model of a well-engineered German camera. Even though his work focused on showing Cuba's leaders as real people, something special happened when he snapped Che's photograph. Somehow Korda had transformed a snapshot into a portrait of someone larger than life.

Luck played only a small role in the making of the *Guerrillero Heroico* photo. Korda brought skills from a previous career to that moment on the memorial stage. Born Alberto Díaz Gutiérrez, Korda took a new name when he opened a photography studio in Havana in the early 1950s. As a successful fashion photographer during the period of the Batista government, Korda had been in the business of making people glamorous. In his busy studio, he photographed models in stylish clothing and elegant poses. "I was the creator of fashion photography in Cuba because, until this very day, I love the female figure," he said. His photographs were published abroad, including in the glossy pages of the American fashion magazine *Vogue*.

Korda, with his skilled fashion photographer's eye, recognized something remarkable as soon as Guevara appeared in the viewfinder. With his powerful 90mm lens, Korda zoomed in to capture the details of Che's wispy beard and glossy coat on the camera's Kodak Plus-X film. Korda knew Che's clothing and hair were not simply fashion choices, but symbols of revolution. His military-style hat was a reminder of a revolution fought. Like Castro's other followers, Che had let his hair and beard grow shaggy to contrast with Batista's clean-cut soldiers. "All the elements are there," Korda said later. "The black beret, the olive jacket, the beard, and long hair."

For the rest of his life, Korda underplayed his role in *Guerrillero Heroico.* "I'm not any kind of genius," he would say. But photography curator Trisha Ziff points out that the photo is actually "very stylized," reflecting Korda's fashion background. Korda made choices beginning with the very moment Che appeared in his viewfinder. "I shot the photo horizontally," he said. "I immediately realized that the image of him was almost a portrait, with the clear sky behind him. I shifted the camera to a vertical [position] and shot a second photo."

Back in the studio, Korda continued to shape the image. Of the two nearly identical photographs of Che, Korda favored the vertical shot. But the top of another man's head over Che's shoulder interrupted the empty background. To get a portrait of Che against a moody sky, Korda cropped the horizontal photograph to make it vertical. It was easy to eliminate the palm fronds appearing to the right of Che's face and the profile of a man on the left. Without tropical plants or the face of Argentine journalist and revolutionary Jorge Masetti, the photo could have been taken anywhere. "You have this image … of a very handsome man, and … you really don't know what you're looking at, so it's filled with mystery," said Ziff.

Korda would later brush off questions about his artistic techniques. He wanted viewers to never forget

Korda's uncropped photo of Guevara included palm fronds and the profile of Jorge Masetti, a journalist and close friend of Che.

why he took that photograph, and others he took while working with Castro. They were documents of Cuba's revolution. He did acknowledge that in his famous photograph of Che "there appears to be a mystery in those eyes." But he went on to say that "in reality it is just blind rage at the deaths of the day before, and the grief for their families."

Korda could describe the emotions that showed on Che's face because he felt them too. The two had more in common than being born in the same year, 1928. Both gave up comfortable lives to dedicate themselves to the revolution. Guevara was a restless medical student when he left his life in Buenos Aires, Argentina, to explore South and Central America. But his journey on motorcycle and on foot gave him more than an adventure. Everywhere he saw the suffering of people in poverty. Che wrote in his diary: "I began to realize at that time that there were things that were almost as important to me as becoming famous or making a significant contribution to medical science: I wanted to help those people." He would ultimately become a Cuban citizen and help lead a revolution to bring down a government that did not seem to care about the poor.

Like Che, Korda couldn't escape the injustice he witnessed. As a fashion photographer, he enjoyed parties with celebrities and drove a Porsche. But he also carried his camera on solo walks through Havana, taking pictures of "things that troubled my heart." He saw people begging and sleeping on streets under newspapers. One image changed his life forever. In 1959 he photographed a girl so poor that she cradled a piece of wood in her arms as if it were a doll. After taking *La Niña de la Muñeca de Palo*, Korda said, "I realized that I had to dedicate my work to this Revolution that promised to erase these inequalities." One of Korda's daughters, Diana Díaz,

"I realized that I had to dedicate my work to this Revolution that promised to erase these inequalities."

Korda holds the photograph that changed his life—*La Niña de la Muñeca de Palo.*

later said about her father: "With the beauty in his images, he did as much as any other person for the revolution and for the poor."

At the memorial service, Korda stood below the prime minister's podium "with the people," as his daughter Diana later noted. Years before the *La Coubre* incident, Guevara himself had helped Korda empathize with the ordinary citizens of Cuba. Korda never forgot traveling to sugarcane fields far from the capital with the assignment of photographing Che working in the fields. Guevara knew Korda was a city boy, raised in Havana, and needed to understand the life of the peasant in order to understand the revolution. "Get the photographer a machete, because he's going to take part in the people's sugarcane harvest," Korda recalled Che's saying. "And I had to spend the next week cutting cane before I could take any pictures."

The photo of Guevara at the memorial service hung on Korda's studio wall for years. But Korda helped to launch his photograph of the revolutionary hero on its global journey. At times he gave prints of the photo to Cuban and foreign guests visiting his studio.

The timing of the photograph's first public appearance in April 1961 was uncanny. The picture was part of an announcement in *Revolución* for a lecture Guevara was to give—a lecture that was canceled because of the Bay of Pigs invasion. Korda had taken the photo of Guevara's defiant face during a speech in which Castro predicted the invasion that happened a year later.

Then Korda's image disappeared from public view, just as Guevara himself did in 1965. Castro read a letter in which Che explained that he had left Cuba to "fight imperialism … in new fields of battle." For two years the world wondered where the restless Guevara had gone.

Korda's photo appeared in magazines outside Cuba in 1967, when news of Guevara's death

STORYTELLER OF THE REVOLUTION

Books by and about Che Guevara are extremely popular in Havana and throughout Cuba.

While Alberto Korda's photograph has made Che Guevara into an unforgettable historical figure, Guevara's own words helped too. When Guevara took an eight-month journey across South America in 1952, he kept a diary. Once back in Argentina, he edited the entries into crafted essays full of humor and criticism of injustice in the world. They were published long after his death as *The Motorcycle Diaries* in 1992.

Guevara kept another diary while fighting in the Cuban revolution against Batista. The new nation enthusiastically embraced his telling of the story that read like a myth. *Episodes of the Cuban Revolutionary War* tells a story of heroes and does not dwell on the most brutal aspects of war.

After Guevara died in 1967, a Bolivian official, Antonio Arguedas, secretly arranged for his diaries to be sent to Cuba the next year. Eager to spread the heroic last chapter of a Cuban hero, Castro rushed to have the writings published. *The Bolivian Diary* became an international bestseller, with Korda's *Guerrillero Heroico* gracing the cover. But readers wanted the full story. Guevara had left Cuba in 1965, and *The Bolivian Diary* began in December 1966. Readers would have to wait more than three decades, until it was published in *The African Dream: The Diaries of the Revolutionary War in the Congo*, to read the missing chapter.

shocked the world. After failing to organize a revolution in Congo, Guevara had traveled to Bolivia to help overthrow its military government. Bolivian troops captured him in a remote village on October 8, 1967, and executed the 39-year-old the next day.

The next year, Korda's lens would find a new focus. Police barged into his studio in 1968 during a crackdown on small businesses to eliminate private property in Cuba. They confiscated most of his photography collection. Small business owners such as barbers and food vendors lost their jobs and many fled to the United States.

Korda did not leave Cuba in 1968, but he turned his lens away from government leaders to photograph undersea life. For a decade he explored the tropical waters around Cuba with an underwater camera. Japan had a major exhibition of his work in 1978, including striking black-and-white images of sculpturelike coral. Nevertheless, his daughter Diana says that her father "made not a single word against the revolution."

Finally, in the 1980s, Korda began to share his photograph's fame. The world learned that the iconic photograph of Che was his. A short documentary by Chilean filmmaker Pedro Chaskel in 1981, for example, featured an interview with Korda about making *Guerrillero Heroico*. Now Korda traveled the world as his photograph had for decades.

Museums and galleries displayed his work. He was interviewed for magazines, books, and documentary films. He described the moment of taking Guevara's photo countless times for audiences. He even wore a gold medallion with a reproduction of *Guerrillero Heroico* around his neck and said, "It will stay with me until I die."

Korda died in Paris on May 25, 2001, while attending an exhibition of his work. He is buried in Havana's Colón Cemetery, just a block from where he had captured Guevara's face 41 years earlier.

ChapterFour:
PORTRAIT FOR THE PEOPLE

Alberto Korda insisted he wasn't trying to make history when he photographed Che Guevara on the memorial stage. He believed his purpose was to record history. About his collection of photographs, he said that "in fifty or a hundred years, there will be people writing about the Cuban revolution, and this [archive] is a historical fact."

But since the world discovered Guevara's portrait in 1967, people on nearly every continent have called it their own. They have found that *Guerrillero Heroico* reflects the frustration, outrage, and defiance they feel in their lives. Many people and events have helped Korda's photo gain and maintain this universal power.

When the larger-than-life revolutionary seemed to disappear in 1965, the world took notice. Che had once traveled the world giving television interviews and speeches at the United Nations. His mysterious absence stirred the imagination of his admirers and enemies alike. In the summer before Guevara's death, Castro gave a speech next to a mural-size copy of the photo. Korda's photograph also appeared on billboards along Cuban roads.

Castro understood the power of positive images to influence people's thinking. His government had

produced thousands of posters to motivate Cubans to work hard in the cane fields, learn how to read, and become teachers. With Korda's photo of Guevara dressed in military-style clothing, Castro inspired Cubans to stay committed to building a new society, no matter the cost.

But when the photograph crossed the Atlantic Ocean, neither Korda nor Castro could control its path. Korda's photograph of Che filled a page in the French magazine *Paris Match* in August 1967. The headline of the accompanying article about guerrilla fighters asked, "Che Guevara. Where

Is He?" The question of who took the photograph went unanswered as well. In small print below the photo, someone had supplied the title *Guerrillero Heroico*. And someone had claimed the photograph. The words "Copyright Libreria de Feltrinelli" declared that it belonged to an Italian millionaire, Giangiacomo Feltrinelli.

Feltrinelli deeply admired Cuba's revolutionary leaders, and he had visited Cuba in 1967 when he was planning to edit a book about Guevara. While searching for a high-quality photo of Che to use in the book, he went to Korda's studio. Korda, who considered Feltrinelli a "friend of the revolution," gave him two prints of his photo of Guevara. He wasn't even bothered when Feltrinelli claimed the copyright of *Guerilla Heroico*. "I still forgive him," he said, "because by doing what he did he made it famous."

Feltrinelli knew he had a powerful portrait—one possibly powerful enough to protect Guevara from harm, wherever he was. Back in Italy, Feltrinelli wanted more people to know about Guevara, and he printed thousands of black and white posters to give away in his bookstores. But by the time the posters arrived in his stores, Feltrinelli's fears had been realized.

On October 10, 1967, the Bolivian government gave the press new photographs of Guevara. Instead of the expressive face of *Guerrillero Heroico*, the world now

Giangiacomo Feltrinelli

saw a disheveled Che lying dead. Bolivian officers and soldiers stood next to his gaunt body, which was marked with wounds. Enraged young admirers of the revolutionary snatched up Feltrinelli's posters from his bookstores and joined demonstrations in the streets of Milan. Italian photographer Giorgio Mondolfo later recalled that "the first time I saw the picture by Alberto Korda, I was not even slightly interested in the author ... it was the picture that had drawn us—many for the first time—to gather in the streets, crying 'Che lives!'"

Nearly a million people attended Guevara's memorial ceremony in Havana eight days later. A print of Korda's photograph hung down five stories of a government building in Havana's Plaza de la Revolucion. The scene inspired a permanent steel sculpture of *Guerrillero Heroico* that marks the place today. At the podium, Castro declared that Guevara's revolutionary ideas "have and will continue to have universal value."

Castro's prediction may not have come true without the help of many artists. There was a newly created poster in the crowd at Guevara's memorial. One of Korda's friends, artist Jose Gomez Fresquet, also known as Fremez, had printed Korda's *Guerrillero Heroico* in ghostly gray ink on red paper. The Cuban government continued to rely on artists, as it did photographers, and it later enlisted artist

Niko's poster of Guevara included the words Castro had spoken at Che's memorial service: *Hasta La Victoria Siempre*—Ever Onward to Victory.

Antonio Perez Gonzalez, also known as Niko, to print an official bold, two-tone poster.

Artists outside Cuba also went to work upon hearing news of Guevara's death. Irish artist Jim

Fitzpatrick is well known for his iconic screen print of *Guerrillero Heroico*. "When he was murdered," Fitzpatrick said, "I decided I wanted to do something about it." He traced a print of Korda's photograph and made stencils on screens and pressed ink through them onto paper. Using this silkscreen technique, he printed Guevara's face in black on vivid red. With a marker, he hand-colored the beret's star in yellow.

With pencils, pens, and printing inks, artists were changing Korda's image. In Fitzpatrick's famous screen print, he made Guevara's hair fuller and adjusted the eyes to look farther into the distance. He even hid an initial of his own name in a curl of Guevara's hair.

Most important, Fitzpatrick and others continued what Korda had done by cropping the original photo. The photographer had removed the palm tree and a man's profile. With silkscreen printing, artists now flattened details of the face into simple shapes. Vivid colors replaced the soft shadows in Korda's image. Art historian David Kunzle explains that no matter how much artists change the image, it remains familiar because of the strong shapes of Che's hair, his beard, and the beret's star.

Fitzpatrick helped Korda's image of Che become the face of anyone's hero. For Fitzpatrick, who lived in Dublin, Ireland, the image represented the Irish Republican Army's fight for freedom from British rule. He wanted his poster to spread the spirit of revolution, not hang in a museum as a precious object. Like Korda, he gave away free copies, sending them across Ireland and beyond, to political groups in England, France, the Netherlands, and Spain. He was pleased with the result. "Months later," he said, "I was over in London and I saw my image everywhere."

Like Feltrinelli and Fitzpatrick, many people continued to spread the Korda image in various forms—not just artists, but anyone with a photocopier. In 1968 *Guerrillero Heroico*, in its many versions, became less about Cuba's struggles and more about protests around the globe.

The assassination of Martin Luther King Jr. in Memphis, Tennessee, caused riots in many U.S. cities. Presidential candidate Robert Kennedy, whose brother, President John F. Kennedy, had been assassinated in 1963, was shot to death while campaigning for the Democratic nomination in California. The controversial Vietnam War raged on during its most violent year. Guevara once wrote about the importance of "feeling most deeply any injustice committed against anyone, anywhere in the world." Throughout 1968 *Guerrillero Heroico* traveled as Guevara had in life—back and forth across the Atlantic Ocean, from one upheaval to another.

People around the world were deciding for themselves what *Guerrillero Heroico* represented and

In 1968 *Guerrillero Heroico,* in its many versions, became less about Cuba's struggles and more about protests around the globe.

Students streamed along a Mexico City street in August 1968 carrying a banner bearing Guevara's portrait. The students were protesting police violence, which later that fall would result in many deaths.

how it should be used. In Prague, Czechoslovakia, people faced the invading Soviet Union's soldiers and tanks with raised posters of *Guerrillero Heroico*. Students in Mexico City clutched the image while protesting the government's killing of unarmed students in a protest.

Fitzpatrick's red and black poster was everywhere during Paris riots that May. Students protested capitalism and the old-fashioned traditions they saw around them by taking over university buildings and fighting police with homemade explosives.

Guerrillero Heroico even traveled to the country where Cuban sugar could not—and no politician could stop it. In Washington, D.C., New York City, Chicago, and Berkeley, California, students carried posters of the image in demonstrations pressing their government to pull troops from the Vietnam War. These so-called "hippies" imagined that Che looked like them. They, too, wore their hair long. They imagined that they felt like him when challenging the war, the political system, and their parents' old-fashioned ways. But by 1968—the year police gutted Korda's studio—the real story of the Cuban revolution was much different from what American young people imagined. Castro even banned long hair, fearing that young Cubans, like American youth, would rebel against his government.

Americans who carried *Guerrillero Heroico* images to strengthen their antiwar message did not know—or tried to ignore—the entire story behind Che Guevara. He believed that violence was necessary to bring about great change. Guevara once said that "a well-aimed shot fired at the right person is much more powerful and effective than the most powerful and effective peaceful demonstration."

Today *Guerrillero Heroico* continues to appear around the globe. And people continue to attach

PROMOTER OF REVOLUTION

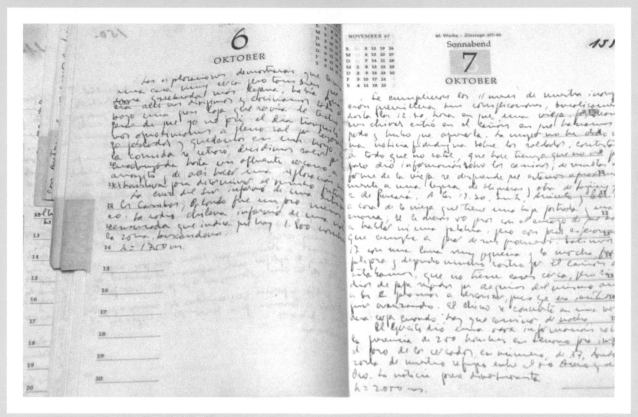

Che Guevara's diaries, which provide detailed accounts of his life, were published in several books.

Born into one of Italy's wealthiest families, Giangiacomo Feltrinelli could have led a quiet life of leisure. Instead he used the money he inherited to fight the injustice he saw in society. Castro and Guevara would help inspire this controversial figure to use words—and later violence—to make revolution.

Tutors taught the young Feltrinelli, who had few friends. His opinions of wealth changed as he got to know the people who worked in his lavish home. He later wrote, "The world, and Italy too, is divided into two kinds of persons: those who have money, land, factories and houses, and those who have no money, and have to work like dogs."

In 1954 he used his wealth to launch a publishing house he hoped would help change society. He caused a stir when he helped smuggle the book *Dr. Zhivago*, by Russian author Boris Pasternak, out of the Soviet Union. Internal politics caused the Soviets to unsuccessfully try to stop him from publishing the book, which criticized the Soviet government.

Feltrinelli admired Cuba's leaders and wanted to tell their stories. He met Castro in 1964, and they became friends. Feltrinelli rushed to Cuba in 1968 to help the Cuban government publish Guevara's *The Bolivian Diary*. His book included a note stating that money from its sale would be donated to "the revolutionary movements of Latin America."

Feltrinelli then moved from books to weapons in his rebellion against injustice. He was known for his creativity in making homemade explosives, and in 1969 he was a suspect in a deadly Milan bombing. Several years later, in 1972, Feltrinelli died in an explosion that he may have accidentally set off while trying to destroy electric power lines. Supporters called him a revolutionary. Critics called him a terrorist.

their own stories to it. According to political scientist
Eric Selbin, it "shows up almost anywhere there's a
struggle." Posters and stencils showing the image go
up on walls in the Middle East, Latin America, and
Europe. "You can make him mean whatever you want
him to mean," Selbin said of Guevara.

Cuba also turned to Che's photo for help. By the
early 1990s, the island was desperate for income. The
U.S. embargo was still in place. The Soviet Union,
Cuba's trading partner for decades, had broken apart.
Cuban leaders hoped to attract tourists with the
iconic image. The government printed *Guerrillero
Heroico* on postcards, T-shirts, and military hats and

sold them to tourists at official stalls around Cuba. Korda's image even appeared on the 3-peso coin, which tourists took home as souvenirs. A former Cuban ambassador to the United Nations, Alcibiades Hidalgo, pointed out that "sale of Che paraphernalia … had nothing to do with the Che's ideals."

As early as the 1960s, people around the world realized that *Guerrillero Heroico* could do more than spread political ideas. Che's dashing face could make money. It made no difference that Guevara himself saw capitalism and business competition as a "contest among wolves." He believed that all citizens should volunteer their time to improve their communities. He worked in the sugarcane fields on the weekends for no pay. He believed everyone should earn the same amount of money, whether a doctor or a farmworker.

But Guevara's beliefs made little difference to business people around the world. From small street stalls to large department stores, businesses made *Guerrillero Heroico* into a familiar symbol that people wanted to wear and own. Though some printed and shared the image for free, others profited. Guevara's face appeared on handkerchiefs, shirts, and sweatshirts. He has helped to sell everything from clothing and food to jewelry and cleaning products. His face has appeared in advertisements for sneakers and fast food restaurants. People even print Korda's image on themselves as a tattoo.

For decades, Korda's image, in all its versions, traveled around the world as if without an owner. No one asked his permission, or paid him for the right to use it. Korda and other Cuban artists viewed their work as a public service to Cuba. For decades Cuba had no copyright laws, which would have allowed artists to control the use of their work by others.

But when a company used *Guerrillero Heroico* to advertise vodka in 2000, Korda believed things had gone too far. "To use the image of Che Guevara to sell vodka is a slur on his name and … his immortal memory," said Korda. By that point he had the legal right to take the company to court. In 1997 Cuba's government had finally signed an international agreement called the Berne Convention for the Protection of Literary and Artistic Works. International copyright law then protected the Cuban works as property of their creators almost everywhere in the world.

Forty years of wandering without restrictions ended for *Guerrillero Heroico* in 2000. Korda won the court case against the alcohol company. He gave the $50,000 he won in the settlement to the Cuban medical system for such things as buying medicine for children. "If Che were still alive, he would have done the same," Korda said. The photographer described how *Guerrillero Heroico* rewarded him in another way: "Life may not have granted me a

Items bearing Che's image are for sale at a souvenir booth in Cuba.

great fortune in money, but it has given me the even greater fortune of becoming a figure in the history of photography."

After his death in 2001, Korda's daughter Diana Díaz took over the struggle to protect Guevara's reputation outside Cuba. She said her father "knew that I would continue with this very big, very difficult responsibility." Her job of managing the use of *Guerrillero Heroico* around the world has been grueling but successful. She said the money she wins in court pays lawyers for new cases against people who misuse her father's famous work.

But some Cuban-Americans want to curb the use of *Guerrillero Heroico* for another reason. They believe people have forgotten the violent history behind the image. They believe Guevara was not a murdered hero, but a murderer himself.

After the revolution, Cubans who were bitter about Batista's cruelty and torture took matters into their own hands and killed Batista's associates. Castro gave Guevara the job of restoring order. Guevara supervised the execution without a fair trial of hundreds of Batista supporters. Opponents of Guevara point to his sometimes cold-blooded speech. Guevara described "hatred as an element of the struggle; a relentless hatred of the enemy, impelling us over and beyond the natural limitations that man is heir to and transforming him into an effective, violent, selective and cold killing machine. Our soldiers must be thus; a people without hatred cannot vanquish a brutal enemy." They have had some success in censoring Korda's image. For example, some Cuban-American groups objected to a car company's use of *Guerrillero Heroico* at a trade show and for replacing the star on Guevara's beret with the company logo. The automaker apologized for using the controversial figure to promote its products.

Another group fears that *Guerrillero Heroico* is being used in a disrespectful way. Guevara's children criticized a fashion designer for creating an expensive bikini with Korda's image repeating in a pattern. "I don't want people to use my father's face unthinkingly," said Aleida Guevara, the oldest of his four children by his second wife. "I don't like to see him stitched on the backside of a pair of mass-produced jeans. But look at the people who wear Che T-shirts. They tend to be those who don't conform, who want more from society, who are wondering if they can be better human beings. That, I think, he would have liked."

Korda's and Guevara's children work hard to protect the photograph that continues to make their fathers famous. But *Guerrillero Heroico* remains controversial, inspiring many opinions among many people living in many kinds of circumstances. Its power to inspire, entertain, and even infuriate might

Alberto Korda will be forever linked to the revolutionary Che Guevara.

be the reason for its survival even 50 years after Korda pressed his shutter on a cloudy March day in the Caribbean.

Timeline

1926

Fidel Castro is born August 13 in Biran, Cuba

1928

Ernesto Guevara Lynch de la Serna is born June 14 in Rosario, Argentina; Alberto Díaz Gutierrez (Alberto Korda) is born September 14 in Havana, Cuba

1959

The Cuban Revolution ends as Castro and his army defeat Batista

1960

Castro's government begins a takeover of private businesses; *La Coubre*, which is loaded with Belgian weapons, explodes March 4

1953

Castro leads an unsuccessful attack July 26 on barracks of Fulgencio Batista's soldiers

1956

Castro, Guevara, and 80 other men head to Cuba on the yacht *Granma*

1961

Castro's forces defeat U.S.-trained Cuban fighters at the Bay of Pigs

1962

President John F. Kennedy places a full embargo on Cuba; the Cuban missile crisis prompts fears of nuclear war

Timeline

1965

The Cuban Communist Party is formed

1967

Bolivian forces execute Guevara on October 9 in La Higuera, Bolivia

1996

Congress passes the Helms-Burton Act, which strengthens the U.S. embargo against Cuba

1997

Cuban government signs the Berne Convention, giving Cuban artists, writers, and musicians international copyright protection for their works

2001

Alberto Korda dies May 25 in Paris, France

1968

Major political events spark protests and riots across North America and Europe

1991

The Soviet Union, which is Cuba's main trading party, collapses, devastating Cuba's economy

2008

Raúl Castro takes over as Cuba's leader after his brother, Fidel, resigns

2015

The U.S. and Cuba re-establish diplomatic relations

2016

President Obama visits Cuba, the first president to do so in 88 years

Glossary

archives—collection of historical documents or records providing information about a group of people, place, institution, or event

barracks—buildings where soldiers live

capitalism—economic system that allows people to freely create businesses and own as much property as they can afford

Cold War—conflict between the United States and the former Soviet Union that did not result in actual war

communism—system in which goods and property are owned by the government and shared in common; communist rulers limit personal freedoms to achieve their goals

confiscate—take someone's property with authority

controversial—causing dispute or disagreement

copyright—the legal right to control the use of works of art, music, or literature and to give permission for its use by others

credit—money borrowed to buy something; the money must be paid back later

embargo—act by a government stopping trade to or from another country

latifundio—large landed estate with agricultural laborers often in a state of partial servitude

recruit—to ask someone to join a company or organization

sabotage—to damage, destroy, or disrupt on purpose

Additional Resources

Further Reading

Engle, Margarita. *Enchanted Air: Two Cultures, Two Wings: A Memoir*. New York: Atheneum Books for Young Readers, 2015.

Hyde, Natalie. *The Cold War and the Cuban Missile Crisis*. New York: Crabtree Publishing Co., 2016.

Wells, Rosemary. *My Havana: Memories of a Cuban Boyhood*. Somerville, Mass.: Candlewick Press, 2010.

Internet Sites

Use FactHound to find Internet sites related to this book. All of the sites on FactHound have been researched by our staff.

Here's all you do:
Visit *www.facthound.com*
Type in this code: 9780756554408

Critical Thinking Using the Common Core

How did the *La Coubre* explosion contribute to the face-off between the United States and the Soviet Union during the Cuban missile crisis? (Key Ideas and Details)

Fidel Castro's government printed Alberto Korda's *Guerrillero Heroico* on billboards. Businesses have used the image in advertisements. How have the Cuban government and private businesses used the image for the same purpose? How have their purposes been different? (Integration of Knowledge and Ideas)

How did Korda's photograph of Che Guevara inspire young people of the 1960s? Who might similarly inspire young people today? What would they appreciate about that person's style and personality? (Integration of Knowledge and Ideas)

Source Notes

Page 4, line 8: "Castro at Funeral for Victims of March 4 Ship Explosion." Castro Speech Data Base. Latin American Network Information Center. 5 March 1960. 2 Feb. 2016. http://lanic.utexas.edu/project/castro/db/1960/19600307-1.html

Page 5, line 2: Ibid.

Page 6, line 1: Ibid.

Page 6, line 18: Stuart Jeffries and Vanessa Thorpe. "The man who gave Che to the world." *The Guardian.* 26 May 2001. 2 Feb. 2016. http://www.theguardian.com/world/2001/may/27/cuba.stuartjeffries

Page 9, line 4: Michael J. Casey. *Che's Afterlife: The Legacy of an Image.* New York: Vintage Books, 2009, p. 46.

Page 9, line 9: Ibid., p. 86.

Page 10, line 19: "Che Guevara photographer dies." BBC News. 26 May 2001. 2 Feb. 2016. http://news.bbc.co.uk/2/hi/americas/1352650.stm

Page 12, line 11: "Castro at Funeral for Victims of March 4 Ship Explosion."

Page 19, line 10: "Castro at Funeral for Victims of March 4 Ship Explosion."

Page 20, line 2: "First Anniversary of the La Coubre Disaster." Castro Speech Data Base. Latin American Network Information Center. 6 March 1961. 16 Feb. 2016.http://lanic.utexas.edu/project/castro/db/1961/19610306.html

Page 22, line 16: Ibid.

Page 22, line 25: *Che's Afterlife: The Legacy of an Image*, pp. 25–26.

Page 23, line 12: "Castro at Funeral for Victims of March 4 Ship Explosion."

Page 28, line 3: "Alberto Korda, Cuban Photographer." Havana Cultura. 16 Feb. 2016. http://havana-cultura.com/en/visual-arts/alberto-korda

Page 28, line 15: *Che's Afterlife: The Legacy of an Image*, p. 82.

Page 28, line 19: Ibid.

Page 31, line 11: "Alberto Korda, Cuban Photographer."

Page 31, line 27: Winifred Yu. "Revolutionary Glamour." *American Photographer.* May 1989, p. 51.

Page 32, line 2: "Alberto Korda, Cuban Photographer."

Page 32, line 4: Sarah Caspari. "Global Perception of Che Guevara." 22 Feb. 2013. 8 Feb. 2016. Pulitzer Center on Crisis Reporting. http://pulitzercenter.org/reporting/famous-photograph-Che-Guevara-Cuba-Argentina-Korda-Castro-Cuban-Revolution-Guerrillero-Heroico

Page 32, line 7: Jorge G. Castañeda. *Compañero: The Life and Death of Che Guevara.* New York: Vintage Books, 1998, p. 195.

Page 32, line 23: "Global Perception of Che Guevara."

Page 33, line 4: Michael Chanan. "Alberto Korda: Ebullient Cuban photographer whose portrait of Che Guevara became an icon for a generation of protest." *The Guardian.* 27 May 2001. 8 Feb. 2016. http://www.theguardian.com/news/2001/may/28/guardianobituaries.cuba

Page 34, line 8: Che Guevara. "On Revolutionary Medicine." *Monthly Review.* Vol. 56, Issue 8, 2005. 8 Feb. 2016. http://monthlyreview.org/2005/01/01/on-revolutionary-medicine/

Page 34, line 20: "Alberto Korda, Cuban Photographer."

Page 34, line 26: Ibid.

Page 35, line 1: *Che's Afterlife: The Legacy of an Image*, p. 318.

Page 35, line 5: *Chevolution.* Directed by Trisha Ziff and Luis Lopez, 2008.

Page 36, line 3: "Alberto Korda, Cuban Photographer."

Page 36, line 25: American Experience: Fidel Castro. PBS. 21 Dec. 2004. 16 May 2016.

Page 38, line 21: *Che's Afterlife: The Legacy of an Image*, p. 316.

Page 39, line 6: "The man who gave Che to the world."

Page 40, line 5: *Che's Afterlife: The Legacy of an Image*, p. 82.

Page 42, line 5: Ibid., p. 113.

Page 42, line 13: "Che Guevara, Jim Fitzpatrick and the making of an icon." *History Ireland.* Issue 4, Vol. 16. July/August 2008. 16 Feb. 2016. http://www.historyireland.com/20th-century-contemporary-history/che-guevara-jim-fitzpatrick-and-the-making-of-an-icon/

Page 42, line 16: "The man who gave Che to the world."

Page 43, line 7: Giorgio Mondolfo. E-mail interview. 18 Oct. 2015.

Page 43, line 19: Ernesto Che Guevara and David Deutschmann. *Che Guevara Reader: Writings on Politics and Revolution.* North Melbourne, Victoria, Australia: Ocean Press, 2003, p. 3.

Page 45, line 2: "Che Guevara, Jim Fitzpatrick and the making of an icon."

Page 46, line 6: Donal Lynch. "Che it again, Jim—the artist behind iconic image." Independent.ie. 2 Feb. 2015. 9 Feb. 2016. http://www.independent.ie/entertainment/che-it-again-jim-the-artist-behind-iconic-image-30951469.html

Page 46, line 22: Hilda Gadea. *My Life with Che: The Making of a Revolutionary.* New York: Palgrave Macmillan, 2008, p. 232.

Page 48, line 24: Che Guevara. "Speech to the First Latin American Youth Congress." 28 July 1960. 9 Feb. 2016. Guevara Internet Archive. https://www.marxists.org/archive/guevara/1960/07/28.htm

Page 49, col. 1, line 10: Gaby Wood. "My father, the literary bomber." *The Guardian.* 18 Nov. 2001. 20 May 2016. http://www.theguardian.com/books/2001/nov/18/biography.highereducation2

Page 49, col. 2, line 8: *Che's Afterlife: The Legacy of an Image*, p.117.

Page 50, line 2: "Global Perception of Che Guevara."

Page 51, line 5: The Associated Press. "Revolutionary Che Guevara Gets Makeover." Cuba News. 7 Sept. 2004. 16 Feb. 2016. http://www.cubanet.org/htdocs/CNews/y04/sep04/17e10.htm

Page 51, line 11: *Che Guevara Reader: Writings on Politics and Revolution*, p. 215.

Page 52, line 10: "The man who gave Che to the world."

Page 52, line 25: "Che Guevera Photographer Dies."

Page 52, line 28: "The man who took Che's 'iconic' picture." *The Irish Times.* 2 June 2016. 9 Feb. 2016. http://www.irishtimes.com/news/the-man-who-took-che-s-iconic-picture-1.311154

Page 53, line 6: *Che's Afterlife: The Legacy of an Image*, p. 316.

Page 53, line 25: Che Guevara. "Message to the Tricontinental." 16 April 1967. 9 Feb. 2016. Che Guevara Internet Archive. https://www.marxists.org/archive/guevara/1967/04/16.htm

Page 54, line 14: Chrisafis, Angelique. "Che, my father." *The Guardian.* 2 May 2002. 16 Feb. 2016. http://www.theguardian.com/world/2002/may/03/cuba.angeliquechrisafis

Select Bibliography

"Alberto Korda, Cuban Photographer." Havana Cultura. 16 Feb. 2016. http://havana-cultura.com/en/visual-arts/alberto-korda

American Experience: Fidel Castro. PBS. 21 Dec. 2004. 16 May 2016.

Anderson, Jon Lee. *Che Guevara: A Revolutionary Life*. New York: Grove Press, 2010.

Casey, Michael J. *Che's Afterlife: The Legacy of an Image*. New York: Vintage Books, 2009.

Caspari, Sarah. "Global Perception of Che Guevara." 22 Feb. 2013. 8 Feb. 2016. Pulitzer Center on Crisis Reporting. http://pulitzercenter.org/reporting/famous-photograph-Che-Guevara-Cuba-Argentina-Korda-Castro-Cuban-Revolution-Guerrillero-Heroico

Castañeda, Jorge G. *Compañero: The Life and Death of Che Guevara*. New York: Vintage Books, 1998.

Castro Speech Data Base. Latin American Network Information Center. http://lanic.utexas.edu/la/cb/cuba/castro.html

Chanan, Michael. "Alberto Korda: Ebullient Cuban photographer whose portrait of Che Guevara became an icon for a generation of protest." *The Guardian*. 27 May 2001. 16 Feb. 2016. http://www.theguardian.com/news/2001/may/28/guardianobituaries.cuba

Che Guevara Internet Archive. https://www.marxists.org/archive/guevara/index.htm

"Che Guevara, Jim Fitzpatrick and the making of an icon." *History Ireland*. Issue 4, Vol. 16. July/August 2008. 16 Feb. 2016. http://www.historyireland.com/20th-century-contemporary-history/che-guevara-jim-fitzpatrick-and-the-making-of-an-icon/

Che Guevara Timeline. History of Cuba.com. 20 May 2016. http://www.historyofcuba.com/history/time/Che-1.html

Chevolution. Directed by Trisha Ziff and Luis Lopez, 2008.

Chrisafis, Angelique. "Che, my father." *The Guardian*. 2 May 2002. 16 Feb. 2016. http://www.theguardian.com/world/2002/may/03/cuba.angeliquechrisafis

Gadea, Hilda, *My Life with Che: The Making of a Revolutionary*. New York: Palgrave Macmillan, 2008.

Gott, Richard. "Poster Boy." *The Guardian*. 2 June 2006. 16 Feb. 2016. http://www.theguardian.com/artanddesign/2006/jun/03/art.art

Guevara, Ernesto Che. Maria del Carmen Ariet Garcia, ed. *The Awakening of Latin America: A Classic Anthology of Che Guevara's Writing on Latin America*. North Melbourne, VIC, Australia: Ocean Press, 2013.

Guevara, Ernesto Che. David Deutschmann, ed. *Che Guevara Reader: Writings on Politics and Revolution*. North Melbourne, Victoria, Australia: Ocean Press, 2003.

Guevara, Che. "On Revolutionary Medicine." *Monthly Review*. Vol. 56, Issue 8, 2005. 8 Feb. 2016. http://monthlyreview.org/2005/01/01/on-revolutionary-medicine/

"Havana Arms Ship Explodes; 100 Die." *Chicago Daily Tribune*, p. 1. 5 March 1960. 16 Feb. 2016. http://archives.chicagotribune.com/1960/03/05/page/1/article/havana-arms-ship-explodes-100-die

"History of Sugar." Sugar Nutrition UK: Researching the Science of Sugar. 2 Feb. 2016. http://www.sugarnutrition.org.uk/sugar-information/history-of-sugar/

Holmes, Stephanie. "Che: The Icon and the ad." BBC News. 5 Oct. 2007. 16 Feb. 2016. http://news.bbc.co.uk/2/hi/americas/7028598.stm

Ismi, Asad. "U.S. Restores Diplomatic Relations with Cuba." Global Research. Centre for Research on Globalization. 26 Feb. 2015. 4 Feb. 2016. http://www.globalresearch.ca/u-s-rstores-diplomatic-relations-with-cuba/5433567

Jeffries, Stuart, and Vanessa Thorpe. "The man who gave Che to the world." *The Guardian*. 26 May 2001. 16 Feb. 2016. http://www.theguardian.com/world/2001/may/27/cuba.stuartjeffries

Leigh, Brandi. "Alberto Korda: The Photographer behind the Face of Ernesto Che Guevara." The Art History Archive. 16 Feb. 2016. http://www.arthistoryarchive.com/arthistory/photography/Alberto-Korda.html

Lynch, Donal. "Che it again, Jim—the artist behind iconic image." Independent.ie. 2 Feb. 2015. 16 Feb. 2016. http://www.independent.ie/entertainment/che-it-again-jim-the-artist-behind-iconic-image-30951469.html

Meltzer, Steve. "The extraordinary story behind the iconic image of Che Guevara and the photographer who took it." The Imaging Resource. 6 June 2013. 8 Feb. 2016. http://www.imaging-resource.com/news/2013/06/06/the-extraordinary-story-behind-the-iconic-image-of-che-guevara

Suddath, Claire. "A Brief History of U.S.–Cuba Relations." *Time*. 15 April 2009. 16 Feb. 2016. http://content.time.com/time/nation/article/0,8599,1891359,00.html

"The United States, Cuba, and the Platt Amendment, 1901." U.S. Department of State, Office of the Historian. 3 Feb. 2016. https://history.state.gov/milestones/1899-1913/platt

Uno Foto Recorre el Mundo (A Photograph Traverses the World). Directed by Pedro Chaskel, 1981. https://www.youtube.com/watch?v=ARnR8yRx1OM

Yu, Winifred. "Revolutionary Glamour." *American Photographer*. May 1989.

Index

About the Author

As a former teacher, Danielle Smith-Llera taught children to think and write about literature before writing books for them herself. As the spouse of a diplomat, she enjoys living in both Washington, D.C., and overseas in such countries as India and Romania. She once lived just a little more than 200 miles (322 km) from Cuba, on the sunny island of Jamaica.